GW01080127

Layout
Markus Koenig mit Helge Tscharn

Distributed in the Untited States and Canada by
Distributed Art Publishers
155 6th Avenue Second Floor
New York, NY 10013-1507

Printed and bound in Germany
ISBN 3-932170-37-7

Zu diesem Buch erscheint eine Vorzugsausgabe
mit einem Foto von Helge Tscharn,
Schuber, numeriert und signiert, 1-50, 5 E.A.
Die Vorzugsausgabe kann im Buchhandel
oder direkt beim Verlag bestellt werden.
ISBN 3-932170-41-5

A special edition with a photograph
by Helge Tscharn
appears in conjunction with this book,
slip case, numbered and signed, 1-50, 5 A.P.
This special edition is available from all bookshops
and can also be directly ordered from the publisher.
ISBN 3-932170-41-5

Als Informations- und
Bezugsquelle für Skateboarding den Titus Magalog:
Tel.: 02 51 - 777 111, www.titus.de

Monster Verlag
Dahlweg 126, 48153 Münster
www.monster-verlag.de

Fordern Sie auch kostenlos unser Gesamtverzeichnis an:

Tropen Verlag
Maastrichter Str. 46, 50672 Köln
Tel.: 02 21 - 49 66 05
tropenvlg@aol.com

ACKNOWLEDGEMENTS

SPECIAL THANKS TO TITUS DITTMANN FOR MAKING THIS PROJECT POSSIBLE.

ALSO THANKS TO BRIGITTA DITTMANN, MARKUS KÖNIG, MICHAEL ZÖLLNER, PATRICK BRUNS, DAVID LUTHER, CARSTEN BAUER, THE WHOLE MONSTER CREW, WOLFGANG PRANTL, LARS UND ARNE LANGGUTH, ALL THE GUYS OUT THERE WHO RISKED THEIR LIFES FOR ME: TONY HAWK, CHET THOMAS, STEVE CABALLERO, LEE RALPH, ARTO SAARI, GEOFF ROWLEY, BUCKY LASEK, ANDREW REYNOLDS, JUSTIN REYNOLDS, JAYA BONDEROV, CHAD MUSKA, OMAR HASSAN, JAMIE THOMAS, ED TEMPLETON, TIM BRAUCH, SIMON WOODSTOCK, SHORTY GONZALES, PETEY MARTINEZ, BOB BURNQUIST, MARK GONZALES, FADI NAJRAS, MUSSA NAJRAS, STEFAN LEHNERT, JONATHAN WRONN, BJÖRN RUBNIKOWICZ, MARKUS "CHAD" JÜRGENSEN, PATRICK ELING, TOBIAS HUNGER, FLORENTIN MARFAING ,JAN WAAGE, K.D. SPAN, VEITH KILBERTH, INGO FRÖBRICH, CARSTEN KRIEG, MURMEL, ROBERT STOYE, CHRIS HEITMANN, SAMI HARITHI, JÜRGEN HORRWARTH, CLAUS HEUWINKEL, MAGIC POMMES MÜLLER, GREGOR FLOTHER, FABIO FUSCO, RICHIE LÖFFLER, SUICIDE WEGNER, ROMAN HACKL, DER ERDBEERMANN, JAN KLIEWER, JULIAN DYKMANS, TURKEY, ROLAND OPPENHEIMER, ANDERS PULPANEK, SEBI, STEFAN SIEMS, VINCENT GOOTZEN, MEHMED AYDIN, HOLGER KROSIGK, BOB JOOST, THOMAS NOVAK, TOMM BEZOLD DA SILVA, MIRCO SUZUKI, MARCO MAIWALD, MICHAEL RADLER, STEFAN BIRCHER, CLAUS GRABKE, MARC MITZKA, DINO BONTEMPI, BENNY MANDELDANNEL, KLAUS FRITZ, VOLKER PETERSEN, DENNIS LANGER, LENNIE BURMEISTER, GREGOR JOSEPHUS, COCKROACH, ALEX JONGEN, TERROR, KELLOGGS, MARTIN V. DOREN, POMMES, TILL KEMNER, STEPHAN GERKENS, ERIK MÖLLER, FIPSI, TOBIAS ALBERT, CHRISTIAN SCHAKERT, OLI BÜRGIN, FLORIAN BÖHM, SASA CERINSKI, THORSTEN SCHMIDT, MARKUS LESSNER, WERNER EGGERS, CHRISTIAN KEIL, JOHN HUNT, HEIKO HAASE, PATRICK AHLFELD, LEO CRAZY LEIFERT, SIMON GEORGE, MANUEL PALACIOS, JOSE' LUIS DE LA ROSA, DANIEL ANDRES, RUBEN RAIBAL, ALL THE SKATERS FROM MADRID, SEIFE, MARC LANGE, NU HEINZEL, HOLGER WILL, THE NÖTZELS, JOHNNY BERTHOLD, HEIKO BALDAUF, TERENCE BOUGDOUR, DANIEL BECK, THOMAS ELSTERMEYER, TILL SPANKEN, TIM LIEBTHAL AND MANY MORE. DIRK VOGEL FOR HIS ARTICLES, FINN HERZOG, ROGER KLEIBER, DAGMAR ZWINGMANN, MARIA, STEPHAN PRANTL, BIRGIT KERGER, ALEX ZIEGLER, STEPHAN ROSE, STEFAN OERDER, MTJA ARSENCEK, TECH LUINGO FROM POW POW, TASSO, BUTTERBÄUCKER, CARTMAN, RUTH STÖCKER, LARS FROM GROOVE ATTACK, ADDITIONAL THANKS TO MARK TERKESSIDIS, CHRISTIAN STORMS, DORIS, ILGA TICK, FRANCESCO, DANIEL BULKOWSKI, ANDREAS NEUKIRCH, NATHALIE HOLZNER, FLACHFOTOGRAFICS AND STEFAN BATSCH FROM LODOWN, J.GRANT BRITTAIN FOR HIS INSPIRATION, BRIAN RIDGEWAY FOR HIS SUPPORT, MARLEY, JENS SCHNABEL, THE GOD OF 8-WHEELS MARTIN BROICH, CARMEN NAGELMANN FOR FLYING CHEAP, SILKE SCHATZ, MAGGY AND YÖRG, GOOFY, OLI MARTEN, CHARLY HANSEN, MONIKA DIEMA, EIKE, PETER U. DORIS PETERSEN, TANJA BANNERT, FRANK KOCH, MARCO SCHMIDT, SHREDCONNECTION, MASON, JÖRG LUDEWIG, MIKE THE SHOPPER, HANSI HERBIG, RUTH STÖCKER AND FRANK WASSERMANN, WINTERNATIONAL, CLAUDIA KLEEFISCH, ASTRID REINBERGER, HANS NIESWAND, RALF CHRISTOPH, ROBBE AND ANNE, DIRK LANGEN, TOM GRUNDMANN AND MÄTES, ZALLE AND ANKE, GEE, ERIC SJOBERG, MY LOVE KRISTINA AND EVERYONE I FORGOT, YOU KNOW WHO YOU ARE....

FRANK HIRATHA I SKATEBOARDER I CALIFORNIA I 1999

JÜRGEN HORRWARTH | OLLIE TO FAKIE | FRANKFURT | 2000

THOMAS GENTSCH | FRONTSIDE BOARDSLIDE | BONN | 2000

OGI DE SOUZA I WORLDCHAMPIONSHIPS / DORTMUND I 1999

RALPH WEGNER I KICKFLIP TO FAKIE I HAMBURG I 1999

DAISY CHAINSAW ▌ FRANKFURT ▌ 1996

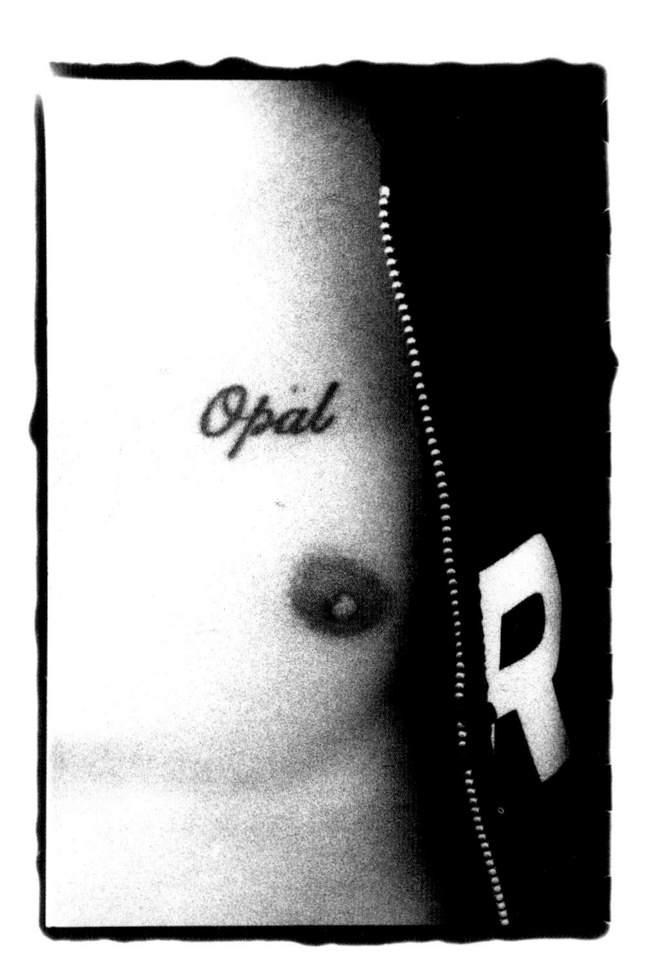

JAMIE THOMAS | SKATEBOARDER | ULM | 1999

MARK GONZALES I WALLRIDE I MUSEUM ABTEIBERG / MÖNCHENGLADBACH I 1998

JULIAN DYKMANS I SKATEBOARDER / MUSICIAN I BRUSSELS I 1999

TOBIAS HUNGER I OLLIE I COLOGNE I 1998

INGO FRÖBRICH | BACKSIDE OLLIE | BONN | 1999

PAUL WELLER / STYLE COUNCIL I COLOGNE I 1996

MONSTER MAGNET I COLOGNE I 1994

FLORENTIN MARFAING | NOSEGRIND | DÜSSELDORF | 1999

ANDERS TELLEN | BACKSIDE TWEAK | COLOGNE | 1999

BJÖRN RUBNIKOWICZ | FRONTSIDE NOSEGRIND | WUPPERTAL | 1999

OLIVER KAHL I NOSESLIDE I BRUSSELS I 1999

REVEREND HORTON HEAT I LUXOR / COLOGNE I 1996

JUSTIN REYNOLDS | BACKSIDE TAILSLIDE | LOS ANGELES | 1998

CHRISTIAN PELZ | FRONTSIDE BLUNTSLIDE | COLOGNE | 1997

DIRK LANGEN | MUSICIAN | BERLIN | 1997

EDWIN COLLINS | COLOGNE | 1996

PRODIGY | COLOGNE | 1996

STEFAN LEHNERT | SKATEBOARDER | LOS ANGELES | 1996

PATRICK AHLFELD | KICKFLIP | MÖNCHENGLADBACH | 1999

BJÖRN RUBNIKOVICZ I FRONTSIDE 50-50 I BRAUNSCHWEIG I 1999

JONATHAN WRONN I FRONTSIDE 50-50 I COLOGNE I 1997

VEITH KILBERTH | COLOGNE | 1999

SAMI HARITHI / MEHMET AYDIN I ISTANBUL I 1998

CHRISTIAN SCHAKERT I BACKSIDE OLLIE I COLOGNE I 1998

TONY HAWK | BACKSIDE OLLIE | ENCINITAS / CALIFORNIA | 1997

MEHMET AYDIN I BACKSIDE TAILSLIDE I BOCHUM I 1998

PHOTEK I LONDON I 1996

JENS SCHNABEL | MÜNSTER | 1997

LARS ULRICH / METALLICA I NEW YORK I 1993

ROB ZOMBIE / WHITE ZOMBIE I LONDON I 1997

MARCUS JÜRGENSEN | FRONTSIDE 180° OLLIE | HAMBURG | 1998

DAMIEN BERBON | FEEBLE GRIND | MONTPELLIER | 1999

FLORENTIN MARFAING I OLLIE I DÜSSELDORF I 1998

KLAUS DIETER SPAN I SKATEBOARDER I BONN I 1993

ROBERT STOYE | FRONTSIDE 50-50 | BERLIN | 1997

ROBERT ELFGEN | ARTIST / SKATEBOARDER | BONN | 1998

HOLGER VON KROSIGK I SWITCH FRONTSIDE TAILSLIDE I AUFMARSCHGELÄNDE / NÜRNBERG I 1998

VICTOR I BACKSIDE 50-50 I PALAST DER REPUBLIK / EAST BERLIN I 1997

ASH | LUXOR / COLOGNE | 1996

TIM DOG | COLOGNE | 1994

TOBIAS ALBERT I MUTE GRAB TO FAKIE I LEIPZIG I 1998

PATRICK ELING | KICKFLIP TO FAKIE | HAMBURG | 1998

VEITH KILBERTH I FRONTSIDE FLIP I COLOGNE I 1998

BACKYARD BABIES | VANS WARPED TOUR / DUISBURG | 1998

VINCENT GOOTZEN I SKATEBOARDER / PAINTER / LAYOUTER I 1998

VINCENT GOOTZEN | KICKFLIP TO FAKIE | MAASTRICHT | 1998

CLAUS HEUWINKEL ▮ OLLIE ▮ COLOGNE ▮ 1998

GOOFY | FRONTSIDE SMITH GRIND | CONNE ISLAND / LEIPZIG | 1998

STEFAN LEHNERT I FEEBLE GRIND I SAN DIEGO I 1997

VEITH KILBERTH I BLINDSIDE OLLIE TO FAKIE I NORTH BRIGADE / COLOGNE I 1998

BOBBY GILLESPIE / PRIMAL SCREAM ❙ COLOGNE ❙ 1997

RIGHT SAID FRED I COLOGNE I 1995

SERGIE VENTURA ■ BACKSIDE METHOD AIR ■ HARDROCK CAFE CONTEST / HOLLYWOOD ■ 1997

DAVE DUNCAN I SKATEBOARDER / RAMPBUILDER / TRAVELLER I 1997

ISTANBUL | 1998

CHRISTIAN HEITMANN | KICKFLIP TO FAKIE | LANDUNGSBRÜCKEN / HAMBURG | 1997

VEITH KILBERTH | BIG OLLIE | COLOGNE | 1997

LARS VEGAS I KARMA / DOPPELGÄNGER / EINZELGÄNGER I COLOGNE I 1997

APHEX TWIN | COLOGNE | 1996

LENNY BURMEISTER | HANDRAIL 50-50 | MÜNCHEN | 1997

ROBERT STOYE | FRONTSIDE 50-50 | BERLIN | 1997

JOHN HUNT ▌ SKATEBOARDER ▌ OSNABRÜCK ▌ 1996

SERGIE VENTURA | BAIL | ENCINITAS / CALIFORNIA | 1997

ROBERT STOYE | SKATEBOARDER | BERLIN | 1998

RICHIE LÖFFLER | FRONTSIDE OLLIE | HAMBURG | 1997

HOLGER VON KROSIGK | SKATEBOARDER | COLOGNE | 1998

MARCO MAIWALD I BACKSIDE 180° OLLIE I COLOGNE I 1997

RALPH WEGNER | FRONTSIDE SMITH GRIND | BRAUNSCHWEIG | 1997

ARTO SAARI | SKATEBOARDER | HELSINKI | 1998

CHET THOMAS I SWITCH FRONTSIDE FLIP I OCEANSIDE / CALIFORNIA I 1997

GREGOR FLOTHER | BACKS DE 180° OLLIE | COLOGNE | 1997

LEE RALPH | ANDRECHT HANDPLANT | ESSEN | 1994

MILLE PETROZZA / KREATOR ❙ ESSEN ❙ 1995

HENRY ROLLINS / ROLLINS BAND ❙ ODEON / MÜNSTER ❙ 1996

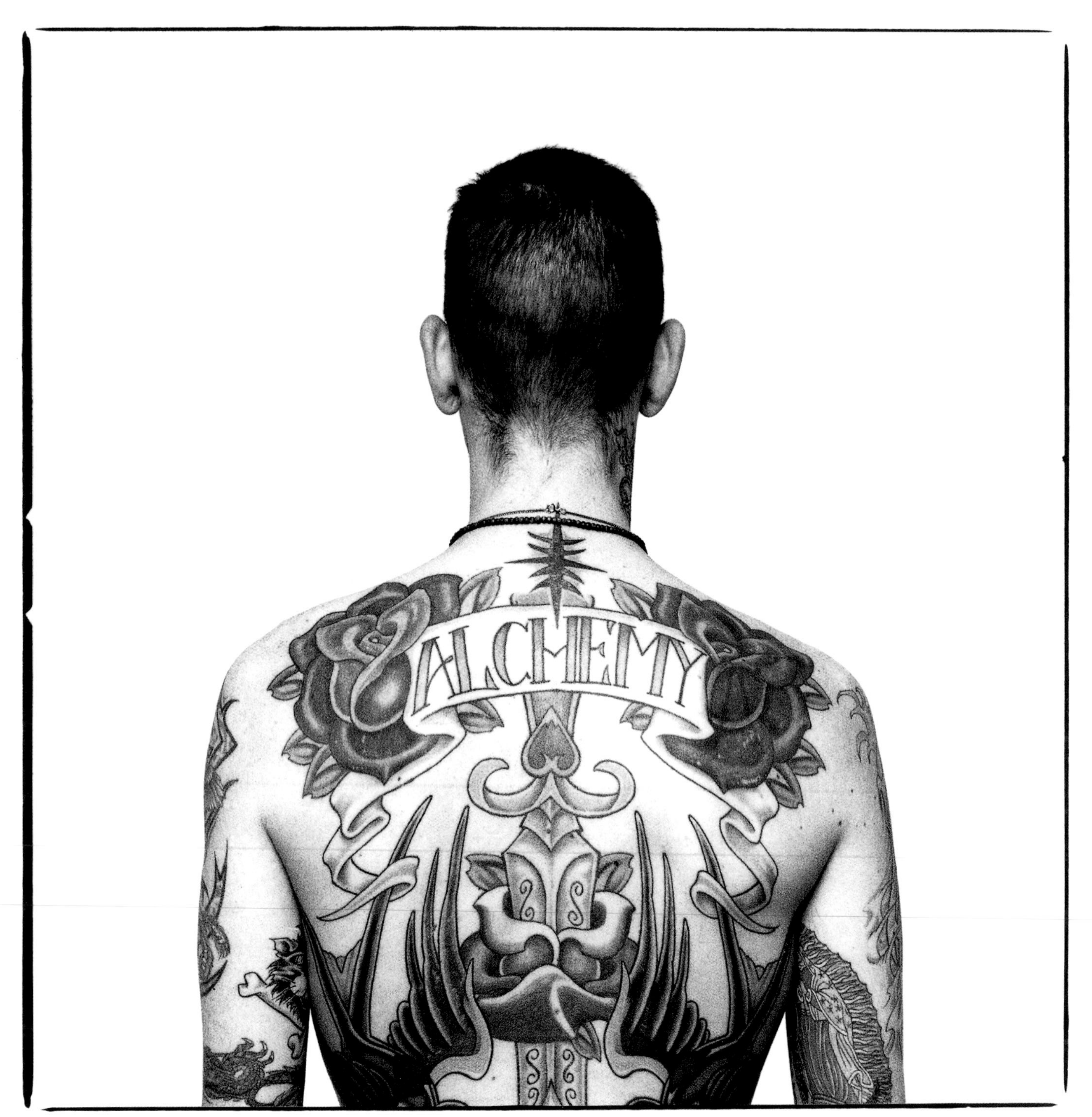

MÄTES I ARTIST I COLOGNE I 1997

SHORTY GONZALES | BACKSIDE 5-0 GRIND | SOUTH CENTRAL / LOS ANGELES | 1996

RÖDELHEIM HARTREIM PROJEKT I COLOGNE I 1996

MARTIN BROICH | FRONTSIDE GRIND | MÜNSTER | 1993

MATT MUFFET | ALLEY OUP EGGPLANT | SAN DIEGO | 1993

CHRISTIAN SEEWALD | FREESTYLER | TITUS SHOW / ST. PETER ORDING | 1993

PIZZICATO 5 | COLOGNE | 1996

ALEC EMPIRE / ATARI TEENAGE RIOT I LONDON I 1995

SAMI HARITHI I OLLIE NOSEPICKER I BERLIN I 1993

MARC MITZKA I FRONTSIDE TAILGRAB ONE FOOT I TROPICA / HEMSBACH I 1993

UNKNOWN | FRONTSIDE GRIND | HAMBURG | 1993

MAD PROFESSOR | COLOGNE | 1997

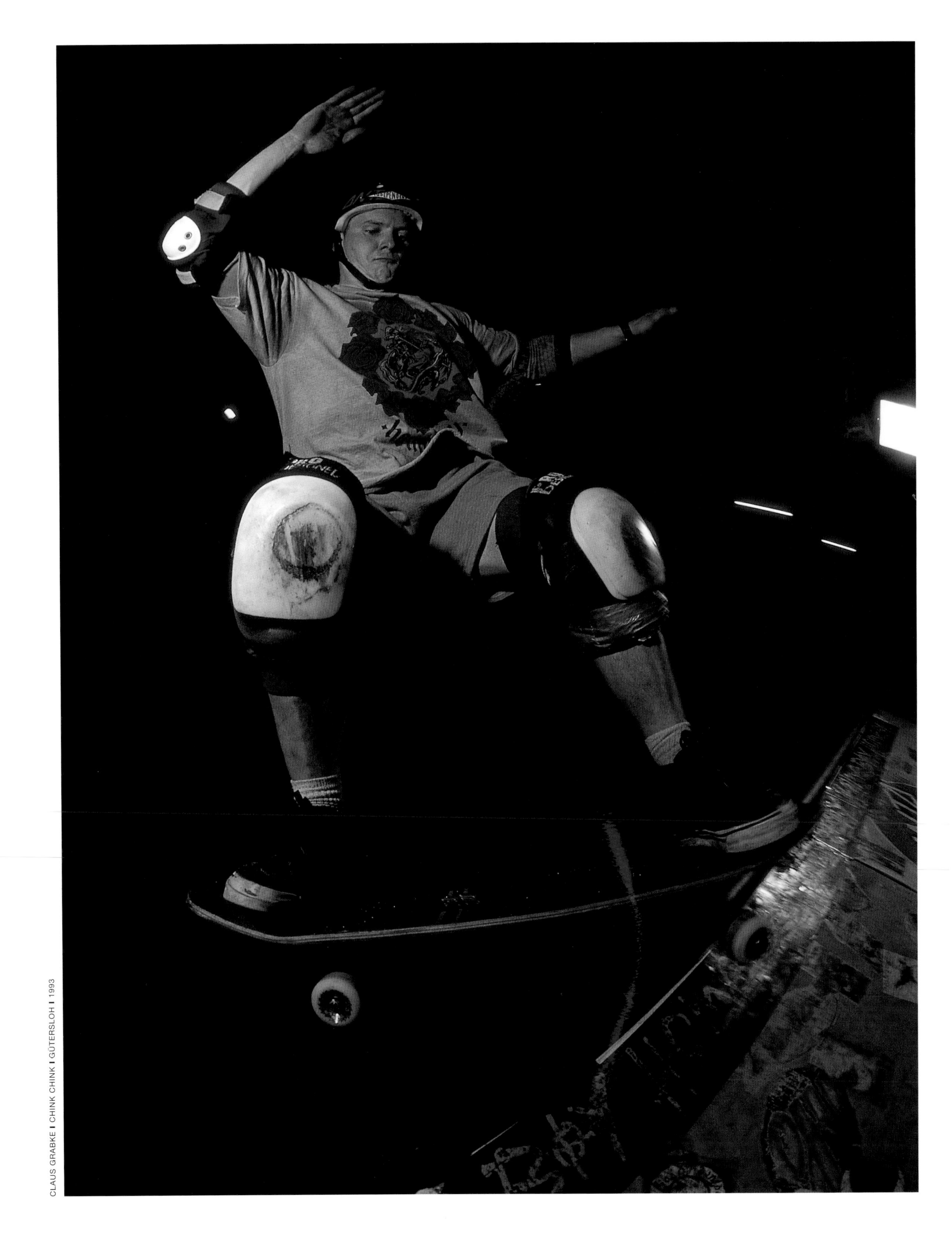

CLAUS GRABKE | CHINK CHINK | GÜTERSLOH | 1993

WADE SPEYER I SKATEBOARDER / LANDSCAPE DESIGNER I SAN FRANCISCO I 1996

ROCKERS HIFI | BIRMINGHAM | 1996

BABES IN TOYLAND I COLOGNE I 1995

GÜNTER MOKULYS | FREESTYLE WORLDCHAMPION | MÜNSTER | 1993

STEVE SAIZ | MC TWIST | MÜNSTER | 1993

THURSTON MOORE / SONIC YOUTH | COLOGNE | 1995

JOHNNY | SKATEBOARDER / MUSICIAN | BONN | 1996

UNKNOWN I FRONTSIDE SMITH GRIND I COLOGNE I 1992

JASON ROGERS ▮ OLLIE TAILGRAB NOSEPICKER ▮ VENICE BEACH / CALIFORNIA ▮ 1992

MARTIN WAGNER I SKATEBOARDER / DANCER / ARTIST I FRANKFURT I 1989

RODNEY MULLEN I OLLIE GRAB I MÜNSTER I 1991

JAMIE LUKA | PIVOT TO FAKIE | STUTTGART | 1991

KEITH MEEK | BACKSIDE LAYBACK SLIDE | SAN JOSE / CALIFORNIA | 1991

MARC SLATER | FRONTSIDE OLLIE | SAN JOSE / CALIFORNIA | 1991

SEAN COONS | FREESTYLER | COLOGNE | 1990

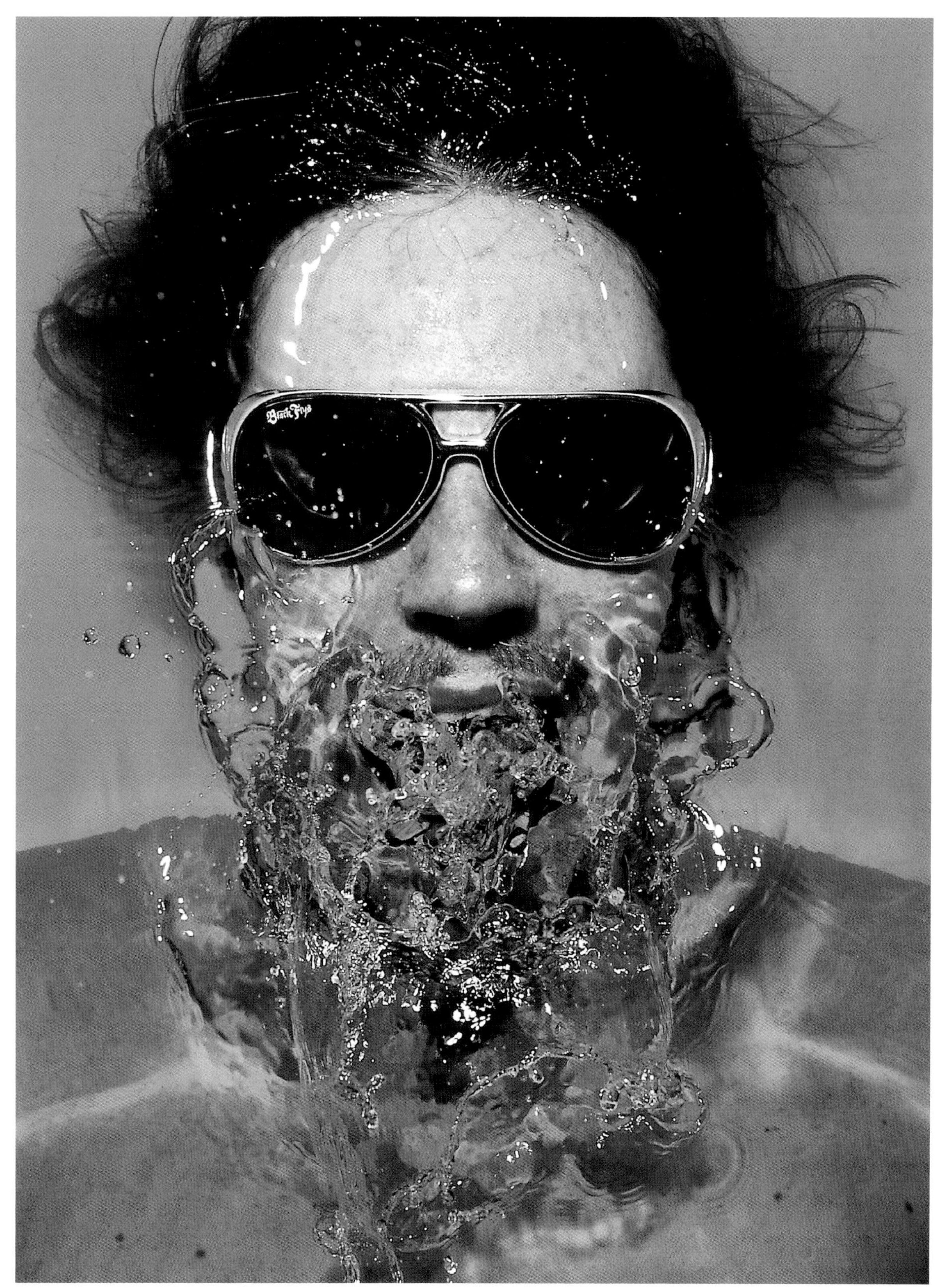

BLACK FLYS I BUBBLES I 1997

BOOTSY COLLINS I 1993

MARTIN VAN DOREN I FRONTSIDE OLLIE I 1991

MIKE MC GILL | BACKSIDE METHOD AIR | ENCINITAS / CALIFORNIA | 1990

ULI NIEWÖHNER I LAYBACK AIR I MÜNSTER MONSTER MASTERSHIP I 1983

CLAUS GRABKE I LAYBACK AIR I MÜNSTER MONSTER MASTERSHIP I 1982

Mark Terkessidis

In Your Face

Die deutsche Musikfotografie war nie sonderlich herausragend. Das lag vor allem an der allgemein stiefmütterlichen Behandlung der Popkultur in der deutschen Öffentlichkeit. Während in Großbritannien Magazine wie "The Face" jahrzehntelang die Zeitschriften-Ästhetik prägten, herrschte hierzulande ein versteinerter Konservatismus bei der Rock-Mainstream-Presse und chronischer Geldmangel bei den Avantgardemagazinen. Im großen und ganzen schienen die Fotos auf eine Funktion beschränkt zu sein: Sie sollten dem Leser von Musikmagazinen oder Illustrierten mal zeigen, wie diese Musikertypen so aussehen. Fotos waren letztendlich Illustrationen für Texte und Interviews. Und etwas anderes wurde auch nicht gewünscht.

Pop-music photography has not distinguished itself in Germany in the past. This was mainly because of the way the German press treated pop culture as a stepchild. While in Great Britain magazines like "Face" have been influencing the aesthetics of journalism for decades, in this country the mainstream rock press was rigidly conservative and avant-garde publications faced chronic financial shortages. By and large, German pop-music photography has seemed to limit itself to one single function: Letting readers of pop-music magazines or articles in illustrateds see what these musician-types look like. Photos have, when all is said and done, merely served to illustrate texts and interviews. And no need has been felt for something more.

Selbstverständlich bleiben Musikfotos in gewissem Sinne immer Portraits, aber ebenso selbstverständlich gibt es unendlich viele Sprachen des Portraitierens. Anfang der neunziger Jahre hat Helge Tscharn seine individuelle Auslegung des Musikfotos eingeführt. Er kam von der Skateboardfotografie und brachte zunächst Geschwindigkeit mit. Seine Aufnahmen wurden schnell geschossen und sollten Dynamik verkörpern.

Naturally, musician photos will always remain portraits; yet the idioms of portraiture are actually infinite. At the beginning of the 1990s, Helge Tscharn introduced an approach entirely his own to pop-music photography. He arrived at this by way of skateboarding photography, bringing with him first of all a new speed. His shots, taken quickly, were intended to embody dynamism.

Am Anfang stand dabei das Fischauge: Der extreme Weitwinkel brachte einerseits die Umgebung des Bandlebens mit ins Bild. Das war meist nicht die Hotellounge, sondern einfach die gekachelte Häßlichkeit fensterloser Backstageräume. Andererseits wurden auf dem Hintergrund des wenig glamourösen Arbeitslebens die Künstler dem Betrachter förmlich ins Gesicht gedrückt. Manches Mal reckten sie sich auch von unten in die Kamera. Gerade Perspektiven wurden durch Accessoires gebrochen – so hielt der Sänger von "Kreator" dem Betrachter einmal ein abgeschnittenes Bein entgegen.

At first, he employed the fish-eye lens. For one thing, its extreme wide-angle let him incorporate the everyday milieu of a band into the picture. The setting was not usually a hotel lounge, but simply the tiled awfulness of windowless backstage spaces. For another, the performers were literally shoved in the viewer's face, against the background of this rather unglamorous working environment. Sometimes they loomed up at you from below. One's line of sight could be interrupted by accessories: once the singer of Kreator even confronted the viewer with an amputated leg.

Helge Tscharn inszeniert verzerrte, tunnelartige Räume, wie sie heute vor allem aus HipHop-Videos bekannt sind. Seine Bilder brachten den Eventcharakter von Popmusik auf die Seiten einer Zeitschrift, die Bilder konnten die zurückgelehnte, geschmackvolle Zeitungslektüre schon mal nachhaltig beeinträchtigen.

Tscharn's aim was a distorted, tunnel-like staging that has become familiar mostly through hip-hop videos. He brought the immediacy of pop music as an event to the pages of German magazines. His images were capable of preventing complacent, tasteful reading. Sometimes the effect could be long-lasting.

Später verschwand das Fischauge, und die Verfremdung der Perspektive inszenierte nun oft die Arbeitsweise der Musiker. Rockers HiFi wurden auf dem Boden fotografiert, die Köpfe in entgegengesetzten Richtungen, aber mit einem Band verschnürt – eine widersprüchliche Produktionseinheit. Den DJ Aphex Twin fotografierte Helge Tscharn durch dessen Hände – im Vordergrund steht nicht der Star, sondern seine Arbeitswerkzeuge.

Subsequently Helge Tscharn stopped using the fish-eye lens, and often achieved the effect of alienation by having the musicians engaged in work-related activities. Rockers HiFi were photographed lying on the floor, with their heads in opposite directions but bound together by a ribbon—a contradictory production unit. The DJ Aphex Twin was photographed by Tscharn through his hands. In the foreground is not the star, but what he works with.

Seit den frühen neunziger Jahren hat sich auch in Deutschland einiges getan in der Musikfotografie. Doch Helge Tscharn war sicher einer der ersten, der dem Musikerportrait eine ganz eigene Sprache gegeben hat.

Since the early 1990s Germany, too, has had something to show in the field of pop-music photography. But certainly Helge Tscharn was among the first to give the musician portrait a language of its very own.

PHIL ANSELMO / PANTERA I COLOGNE I 1995

Johann Christoph Maass

"Everything that's done today will be tomorrow's curse." *Kerry King [Slayer], 1994*

Am Anfang steht das Ereignis. An die Intensität dieses Moments reicht nichts heran. Ein Bild, auf dem Tony Hawk zu sehen ist, während er einen 540° macht, ist nicht Tony Hawk, der einen 540° macht. Dennoch kommt die Fotografie dem Versuch, einen Augenblick zu reproduzieren und ihn für die Nachwelt zu konservieren, am nächsten, auch wenn es sich um ein Abbild der Wirklichkeit und eine Interpretation des Fotografen handelt.

Skateboarding lebt von Bildern, deren Funktion es ist, spektakuläre Momente festzuhalten, Geschichten zu erzählen und das im Foto manifestierte Gefühl an andere weiterzugeben. Für die Fotografierten selbst sind die Fotos Erinnerungen an gute und schlechte Tage, an Schmerzen und Freude. Für die übrigen eine Möglichkeit, etwas von der Faszination dieses Sports und des dazugehörigen Lebensstils zu erfahren. Um die Aura eines Ereignisses erahnen zu können, muß man die Bilder für sich sprechen lassen, sind sie doch Artefakte, die im entscheidenden Bruchteil einer Sekunde entstehen. Sie bilden nicht nur den Akteur ab, sondern berichten auch vom Fotografen als Chronisten: die beiden einzigen, die im Moment des Ereignisses unmittelbar involviert sind.

Und involviert ist Helge Tscharn schon lange. Er hat die Entwicklung des deutsch-europäischen Skateboardings seit ihren Anfängen zu Beginn der achtziger Jahre mit der Kamera dokumentiert, und sein Stil bereichert die Skateboardfotografie seit fast zwanzig Jahren.

Dieses Buch ist das Ergebnis harter Arbeit. Es belegt einen langen, ereignisreichen Weg. Es ist eine Retrospektive, die Einblick in Helge Tscharns bisheriges fotografisches Schaffen bietet, ein Manifest künstlerischer Brillanz als Resultat langjähriger Erfahrungen und Besessenheit vom Sujet. Und es ist eine Hommage an Helge Tscharn, der es mit seinem Stil zu einem der besten Skateboardfotografen weltweit gebracht hat. Wie recht Kerry King von Slayer hatte: "Everything that's done today will be tomorrow's curse." So ist es auch bei Helge Tscharn. Was er heute anfaßt, setzt Maßstäbe für morgen und macht es der Konkurrenz dadurch nicht gerade leicht.

Wie das Foto nicht dem Ereignis, so wird das Wort hier nicht der Wirklichkeit des Bildes gerecht. Es spricht seine eigene Sprache, steht für sich selbst. Der Fotograf ist es, der seinen Bildern Ausdruck und Handschrift verleiht. Lassen wir deshalb die Bilder zu Wort kommen und durch sie Helge Tscharn.

The event comes at the very beginning. Nothing can match the intensity of this moment. Granted, an image in which you see Tony Hawk executing a 540° is not Tony Hawk actually executing a 540°. Still the photo comes closer than anything else in reproducing a momentary event and preserving it for posterity, even if it only reflects reality and involves a photographer's interpretation.

Skateboarding lives through images: Images whose function is to capture spectacular moments, tell stories, and to communicate a certain feeling to others. Those who have been photographed skateboarding can recollect good days and bad ones, remember their pain and joy. Photos allow the rest of us to experience something of the fascination of this sport and its lifestyle. But to experience the aura of an event, you must let the images—mere artifacts created in a fraction of a second at just the right moment—speak for themselves. Photos are not just images of a skater; they also report on the photographer as a chronicler.

Helge Tscharn has been involved in photographing skaters for quite some time. His camera has been documenting the development of German and European skateboarding since its beginnings in the early 1980s. And during all this time, his style has exerted its enriching influence on skateboard photography.

Hard work has gone into the present book, which has been years in the making and taken many twists and turns. It is a retrospective offering a look into Tscharn's photographic work to date, making clear how his artistic brilliance has arisen from long experience, and from being obsessed with a subject. And it is an homage to a man whose style has made him one of the best photographers of skateboarding in the world. "Everything that's done today will be tomorrow's curse." How right Slayer's Kerry King was, and the same applies to Helge Tscharn. Everything he touches today sets the standard for tomorrow, making things a bit tougher for other photographers.

Just as a photo does not do justice to the event it records, so here words do not capture the reality of the images being presented. They have a language of their own, exist in their own right. The photographer has endowed his work with expression and his signature. Let us give these photos the chance to speak, and through them, Helge Tscharn.

INTRODUCTION

JONI WRONN | SKATEBOARDER | 1995

POSSESSED

HELGE TSCHARN

MONSTER VERLAG / TROPEN VERLAG

SELFPORTRAIT | WITH MARC LORENZ | 1987

DEDICATED TO
HEINRICH KLEIBER

SPEED I 1984

POSSESSED